To: Eleanor...
Warmest wishes,
Ed Eisen

A Memoir

Front Row Seat

Ed Eisen

Front Row Seat
Copyright © 2019 by Ed Eisen

All rights reserved
Published 2019

Library of Congress Cataloging-in-Publication Data

No part of this publication may be reproduced, stored in a retrieval system or transmitted in any form by any means without permission of the author.

Front Row Publishing
Jenkintown, PA 19046
www.edeisenshow.com

Eisen, Ed 1936 -
Front Row Seat / Ed Eisen

ISBN: 978-0-578-52092-6

Printed in the United States of America

Cover Design: Integrative Ink
Back Cover Photo: Courtesy Bob Kravitz

Dedication

To my wife, Marion, my companion, my inspiration, my love. A true helpmate. She has worked tirelessly, never abandoning her faith in what I could do. Her inspired editing made this book what it is. To my family, Gwen, Seth, Stacy and Stephen, the real fruits of my labors. To John McCandlish Phillips, my *New York Times* mentor, who continued to encourage when the valleys appeared steeper than the mountain tops.

Table of Contents

Introduction 1

Part 1 Front Row Reservation

1 In the Beginning 7

2 Radio Tales 11

3 The Proposition 15

4 My NY Times Mentor 21

5 Saturdays With Bill 25

6 Gone Girl 29

7 Girl Found 33

8 Costly Transformation 37

9 My Mishpocha 41

Part 2 The Harvest

10 Pope's Jewish PR Guy 55

11 Chicken Soup With Mother Teresa 59

12 The Mafia and Me 63

13 The Millionaire 67

14 Joe Frazier's Glove 71

15 A Beautiful Mind 75

16 The Warehouse 79

17 America's Gandhi 83

18 Jackie Gleason's Send-Off 87

19 Lion of the Senate 91

20 Hangman's Noose 95

21 Bag Lady 99

22 Dating Christine 101

23 Feds Flunk Security Test 105

24 Town Going Dry 109

25 Mass Murderer 111

26 Big Bank, Bad Loans 113

27 Hot TV News 115

28 Spitballs Flying.. 119

29 Before Bandstand 123

30 Lessons Learned.. 127

About The Author 131

Index 133

Introduction

This book is about the people and places I met and visited as a journalist, publicist, and broadcaster. Here you'll meet some of the world's most famous, most infamous characters. The experiences I recount from my 52 years on the road could fill volumes. Instead, each vignette has been cast in but a few pages.

I consider myself lucky, blessed. Why? Over the years my circuitous career can be summed up in a word: *communications*. As a journalist, I focused my spotlight on good institutions and bad actors. I worked as an investigative reporter, business, features writer, and editor. I was a newscaster, top-40 DJ, TV producer and taught broadcast news journalism at Temple University. I've been a talk-show host, public-relations consultant, advertising executive, entrepreneur and motivational speaker.

Among those you'll meet in this remembrance:

- Mother Teresa, the nun from the streets of Calcutta whose gift of insight prompted this skeptic to redirect his purpose
- Joe Frazier, the world-boxing champ, who presented me with the glove that cost him his bout with George Foreman
- John Forbes Nash, Jr., the once certifiably mad Nobel Laureate who understood why the nation's mental health system is failing
- Comic Jackie Gleason who handed me the most humiliating moment of my newspaper career
- Ted Kennedy, the Lion of the Senate, a presidential wannabe whose aspirations were dimmed in the still waters off Chappaquiddick Island
- Bipin Shah, the multi-millionaire who spent $3.2 million to search the world for his missing daughters
- *Bandstand's* first record runner

You'll visit:

- Pennsylvania's House of Horrors where humans were warehoused in secret
- The town where showers were rationed
- Philadelphia's second largest post office and courthouse ripe for the work of a terrorist
- The big bank with risky loans forced to sell its assets

Some have asked: "So how did you get there? How did you acquire your *Front Row Seat?*" Part I of this remembrance transports you to the beginning, the 9th floor tenement where I grew up in mid-30s Brooklyn as America was recovering from the Great Depression. You'll meet folks whose lives over the years were intertwined with my own: a father, a mother, a brother I never met, a beloved cousin who mysteriously disappeared. All speak clearly about the human condition. They, too, have stories, stories compelling and worth telling.

Part II is a collection of my most memorable tales as a journalist for two of Philadelphia's largest dailies. Others represent stories that captured headlines from my years in the weird and wacky world of public relations. Finally, you'll read about a road less traveled my wife and I took that transformed our lives.

Part 1

Front Row Reservation

1
In the Beginning

I have always had more questions than answers. As a kid, that got me into trouble. Once the father of a girlfriend ended our relationship because I probed too deeply about his political preferences. Teachers, politicians, or people in power were often rattled when I drilled down too far. I believe the genesis of my curiosity began when I was five living with mom and pop on a 9th floor tenement in Brooklyn.

I was playing a coin toss with a neighbor, Heidi Singer, at the entrance to 1220 East New York Ave. Heidi dropped a couple pennies onto the street. I gathered them up and clenched the find within my tiny fist.

In tears, she ran to her father. "That boy stole my money!" Stanley Singer, the butcher, was standing with a group of men. My pop, the janitor, was a few feet away.

"Where's your father?" Singer asked. "Why?" I stared at him with puppy-dog eyes. "Cause you're a little thief!" he yelled. "Now where's your father?" I pointed over to my pop.

"Your son stole my daughter's money," the man shouted. My pop was the diminutive bald-headed figure in the crowd, a Polish refugee.

The next thing I saw were two men, fists drawn. They began jousting, like lightweights in a boxing ring. A crowd gathered. I took a seat on the steps near the entrance to our apartment. The butcher landed a jab to my pop's jaw. When Billy Eisen fell to the concrete pavement, a woman screamed. "Call the cops!"

I remember sitting there absorbed like a spectator in a ringside match. "Call your mother!" the woman hollered again. Suddenly it struck me: *Hey, that's my pop on the ground. And he's bleeding.*

"Go get your mother!" the woman yelled again.

I flew up all nine flights to summon mom. She rushed down with a broom. It was too late. An ambulance, sirens blazing, was on its way to the hospital. Pop was inside.

That same year I provoked an uproar in Mrs. Shoemaker's first grade class at P.S. 125, a class of mostly Jewish and Italian immigrant children flooding into Brownsville from New York's Lower East Side. Mrs. Shoemaker asked her young charges to recite — one by one — all vegetables known to man. Tiny hands flew to the ceiling: peas, spinach, onions, celery and more, a chorus of shouts erupted.

Then, timidly, I raised my hand. Mrs. Shoemaker recognized me: "Merelich," I said, trying to muster confidence.

"What in heaven is that?" she asked, appearing as if stung by a wasp. The sound uttered somehow didn't fit the proper English lexicon to which my teacher had grown accustomed. It was a word known to most children of Jewish immigrant parents. It meant *carrots*. A burst of laughter erupted in the room. Then came the thunderous reaction from Mrs. Shoemaker. I was ordered to the front of the class. There she proceeded to yank my crop of red hair.

"Don't you ever dare make fun of me again," she admonished. I stood there trying to hold back the tears. The principal ordered my mother to come in. It is a moment still frozen in time for me. "What did I do wrong?" I prodded the principal.

A week later Mrs. Shoemaker carted a big cardboard box into class. Inside was a huge chocolate cake. To this day I can still taste the moist, fudgy slice she plopped onto my paper plate. The fresh aroma teased my senses along with the smile that lit my teacher's face. Alas, all was well in the world. And it was then that I acquired my life-long love affair with chocolate.

2

Radio Tales

World War II was winding down. My father found work as a welder at the New York Shipyard in Camden, NJ. We moved to nearby Collingswood, a place where tastefully designed apartments were rising like daisies on spacious, green lawns. The contrast to the crowded streets of Brooklyn was stunning. Mom, who sold apples on the streets of Latvia at 5 and pop, raised on a one-cow dairy farm in Poland, had never seen anything like this. Moving with us was my Aunt May, my mom's younger sister, and her son, my Cousin Dick. Television was a decade away from arriving in American households. For entertainment there were the 10-cent movies on a Saturday and the radio. I was an avid radio buff. The Lone Ranger, Superman and his alter ego, Clark Kent, reporter for *The Daily Planet*, provided a playground of imaginative pursuits. I felt lucky. Not bad for a kid whose only toy was a broken cuckoo clock plucked from a trash can.

Cousin Dick and I became active participants in the daily radio soaps. It all started with a couple dozen milk crates. Wooden boxes, repositories for fresh quarts of pasteurized milk that somehow appeared miraculously on our doorstep each morning. The milkman would drop off the empty crates along a traffic island in the Fairview section of Collingswood.

We would pile the boxes into an igloo-like rectangle that mirrored a little kid's vision of a radio station control room, housing a toy microphone and a headset. It was there just a mile from the Black Horse Pike from where Frank Sinatra once performed that Dick and I got our start. We would parrot the deep baritone of announcer Fred Foy: *A fiery horse with the speed of light! A cloud of dust and a hearty 'Hi-Yo, Silver!' The Lone Ranger!* I imagined the clatter of hooves and Rossini's "William Tell Overture" pounding away in the background.

At 7, it was easy to morph from one pipe dream into another. In 1948, fiction became reality when a sports writer from *The Camden Courier Post* spoke at our 8th grade class at Hatch Jr. High School in the Parkside section of Camden.

Here was this nattily attired real-life Clark Kent recalling how the Philadelphia Eagles had become the National Football League champs during a blizzard; how Citation wound up as the 8th horse to win the Triple Crown and how Joe Lewis knocked out Jersey Joe Wolcott in the 11th round to win the world boxing title for the 25th time.

I was hooked by the tales of this reporter whose name I can't remember. What I do remember are the words of my elementary school teacher telling our class that someday "you'll discover your gift, a gift," Mrs. Mills insisted, "was God-given. When you discover it, I hope you'll use it wisely."

I was lucky. Short, freckle-faced, nerdy, I knew what I wanted to do before my Bar Mitzvah. By the time I entered 9th grade, I was named editor of the school magazine. A year later Camden High School's *Castle Crier* listed me on its masthead as editor.

When I turned 16 a traumatic incident helped define me. But it nearly cost my life. One day I was visiting at the home of David Rabinowitz, a school friend. As a kid, David was an avid collector of Broadway show tunes "Can I borrow your *Guys and Dolls?*" I begged. "Ask my mom." he suggested with hesitation.

Sarah Rabinowitz was setting the table for dinner. "Can I borrow David's album?" I pursued gingerly. "No, you may not," came the terse response.

"Why? I asked. "I'll bring it back tomorrow."

"I said no," she shot back, her face flushing red.

"Pretty, please," I persisted.

Mrs. Rabinowitz flew into a rage. She grabbed a carving knife from the table, lunging at me. Sarah's husband was standing just behind her. Instantly Saul Rabinowitz lifted her arms from behind, high, high above her head. The knife fell, slipping to the carpet. In panic, I fled from the house.

Was I traumatized? Probably, but the near tragic event carried a message. I learned something about myself, a lesson that has opened more than a few closed doors throughout my life.

I have made it a practice not to surrender easily. Beyond bold-faced curiosity, persistence is in my DNA. I have virtually discounted every rejection life has tossed at me. Eventually, I wound up with at least one *yes* after scores of *no's*. I've been thrown out of more than a few corporate offices. But my life has never been so imperiled again as my experience with Sarah Rabinowitz. I have attributed my success not to any superior writing skills. But rather to my willingness to knock more than once. Thirty-two years later when I started my own business, I learned the meaning of cold calling. In a 10-hour work day, I would often make 100 calls to achieve one *yes*. And the *yes* didn't translate to a new client. All it meant was that I could drop by to make a presentation.

In 1954, when I graduated from Camden High School, the yearbook entry read: "Ed Eisen, future Ollie Crawford." Crawford was *The Philadelphia Inquirer's* vaunted front-page poet-in-residence.

Writing opened many doors. I was invited to do a weekly radio show on WCAM in Camden, an innovative program to give students an opportunity to report school news. So there I was --finally -- using not a toy but a real microphone to broadcast news to a real audience. And there wasn't a milk crate in sight!

3

The Proposition

My father's education ended in the sixth grade. That's when his parents put him aboard a ship bound for America to escape the creeping Nazi threat invading Europe after World War I. Billy Eisen never saw them again.

He brought with him a small suitcase and a gold watch. Two weeks later pop disembarked at Ellis Island. The watch was gone and Billy headed for Detroit.

He was 11.

He slept in Uncle Herman's varmint-infested basement. Pop hated school. A year later he ran off. My father lived the hobo life for several years hopping freight trains, crisscrossing the country, making do with trash-can waste. Pop married at 16. A year later, fibbing about his age, he enlisted in the U.S. Army, leaving behind his new bride, two months pregnant. Ten months into battle pop was wounded and returned to the states.

His new wife died during child birth, felled by an outbreak of Spanish influenza. A son, Samuel, was born with a medical abnormality, a pinhole in his heart. Pop, unable to care for the infant, placed him in an orphanage. Later Samuel went on to become a civil engineer, repaying his dad for his college tuition. Samuel died at 58, blind and felled by a heart condition that could have been operable.

I never met my brother, a mystery that haunts me to this day, a family secret that pop carried to his grave.

Billy Eisen was 35 when he married Lillian Koppel, my mother, an immigrant from Riga, Latvia. That was the time pop was working as an orderly in a Brooklyn hospital. During World War II when I was six, my parents moved to South Jersey.

By the time I was 11, I would tag along to lift chairs onto desks, swish a mop and run a buffing machine. Pop punched a clock and hung his hat at a place called City Cleaning Co. at 401 N. Broad St. Twelve years later I would hang my hat just across the street at *The Philadelphia Inquirer*.

With pop's earnings and my mom's acumen for saving a penny, my dad presented me with a Smith Corona typewriter soon after I entered junior high school. For me, it was a treasure from which I banged out my first school play and my first news story.

When I started my freshman year at Temple University, pop came home with a *proposition*, as he called it. Those words still ring in my head. "Eddie, my boss has made us a wonderful offer. George Cohen wants to retire soon. He wants to sell us his business. Would you come in with me?" I remember pop's pitch: "You won't have to mop floors. You'll be the front man. You'll bang on doors and sell our work to companies all over the city. Your English is good and the office cleaning business is hot!"

Now you have to understand my pop. Billy Eisen was a head-strong man, very proud, given to outbursts of rage for real or imagined insults, many of which came from my mom. Lillian Eisen was a diminutive woman raised by a grandmother. Soft-spoken, often depressed, her words could be biting.

She had a penchant for asking questions that often impugned her husband's judgment. The acrimony was endless. Once pop yanked a table cloth from the dining room table at Passover. Dishes flew and Billy Eisen disappeared for three months. Mom was near death at 73, diagnosed with pancreatic cancer. I remember pop crying: "I love her so much I would drink her bath water."

My father also possessed an enormous capacity to love, to cry, to cherish those closest to him: his son and his four grandchildren. He would appear at our front door weighted down with bags of candy, cookies, potato chips.

His lack of education didn't keep him from excelling. He read *The Inquirer* daily, relishing a good political debate. He was a gifted speaker, exhorting worshippers to give more generously. Never trained as a cantor, he was hired to conduct worship services at Orthodox synagogues all over West Philadelphia. An article in the old *The Philadelphia Bulletin* described Billy Eisen as a "cantor without portfolio." Code words for son of a cantor who was self-taught.

And so there was my father, home from work on this Monday morning. He sat at the table sipping the tea mom had set before him. His hands were calloused, gnarled, offering silent testimony to his years of hard labor. He repeated again his proposition: He wanted me to join him in the business of cleaning office buildings.

"Pop, I said, "you don't understand. I want to write for a living. I don't see any future in cleaning."

I could see the old man was visibly crushed. The look of excitement quenched from his face. Yet my father had taken a life path brimming with disappointments. This was just another. He said goodnight and went to bed. It was 8 a.m.

My earliest passion was to study at the Pasadena Playhouse in California. Perhaps write a screen play. That was not to be. I worked at a string of radio and TV stations from Florida to New York and in a few years my resume had more holes than a slice of Swiss cheese. The world of broadcasting — then and now — is a pretty fickle place. Better voices, prettier faces are forever nipping at your career longevity.

Ultimately, I found my passion in print journalism. I labored in the vineyards of ink for 15 years at some of the country's major metropolitan newspapers: *The Philadelphia Inquirer,* the former *Philadelphia Bulletin* and a paper once called *The Ft. Lauderdale News,* now Florida's *Sun-Sentinel.* Once established as a journalist — not a DJ —opportunities started piling up from radio stations seeking local material from legitimate news gatherers: print reporters.

From my *Front Row Seat*, I wrote about big town and small town movers, shakers, dreamers, and crooks. Compensation was poor but the psychic income was huge. *Inquirer* Publisher Walter Annenberg paid me $12,000 a year in 1971 when I left the paper to enter public relations. In 2019 reporters at the paper averaged $57,700 annually.

Lawyers, barbers, and pharmacists are not normally recognized for their achievements. Some journalists are. I received two Pennsylvania State Publishers Association awards and another from the Freedoms Foundation.

In all, it was a great career with but one exception. After *The Bulletin* closed in 1982, I was hired as an editor at *The Atlantic City Press*. I was 48 and failed miserably, dismissed over my inability to come up to speed on the company's new computer system.

To this day the sobering words of Publisher Chuck Reynolds rings in my ears: "I'm sorry, Ed. I'm sure you'll be successful at something else." He was right. Had that door not closed I would never have found the courage to become an entrepreneur. I launched my own public relations consulting firm, a company that remained open for 28 years until my retirement. It was in that role that one of the most significant projects of my career came about: recovery of the missing daughters of electronic payment systems architect Bipin C. Shah. (See Chapter 13)

Other clients included some of Philadelphia's most prestigious law, accounting, and architectural firms. Hospitals and health care practices came aboard. I produced a weekly show for WCAU-TV called *The Flower Man*. It delivered several million dollars-worth of free promotion for the Delaware Valley Florists Association.

And so it was in my role as both a journalist and later a publicist that I came to acquire a *Front Row Seat*. For the uninitiated there's a world of difference between journalism and public relations. The job of a journalist is to tell the story and offer opportunities for both sides to be aired. A public relations consultant has the singular mission of representing the client who writes the check.

Think criminal defense attorney. Should you find yourself charged with murder and you have the resources to hire a good lawyer, be assured your attorney will *spin* a defense to achieve a not guilty verdict. The publicist — depending on his or her work ethic — provides a point-of-view designed to present the client in the most positive light. Those who practice crisis management are highly valued by corporate America. Think oil spill and pharmaceuticals that kill. Good publicists are good not because of superior writing talent. Their skills are in sales, pitching a story with scoop potential to a reporter.

My earnings as a PR consultant far outpaced my income as a journalist. But in the end, I sorely missed the 4th Estate. Truth be told, the higher income didn't deliver *greater happiness*. We continued to live and rear our four children in the same twin home in Northeast Philadelphia for 46 years. An earlier book about my travails in the world of public relations was aptly titled: *Soul for Sale – Confessions of a Philadelphia Spin Doctor*.

4
My NY Times Mentor

John McCandlish Phillips, a veteran *New York Times* reporter, who wrote one of the most famous articles in the newspaper's history, was my friend and mentor.

I met John on a business trip to Manhattan when I was working as a spokesman for Pope Paul VI. John's story exposing the Orthodox Jewish background of a senior Ku Klux Klan official grabbed my attention. I had been working in public relations for several years and I was seeking his counsel on how I could ease my way back into journalism. Editors look with suspicion on journalists who have left the profession, moved into PR and seek reentry into the 4th Estate.

One would think a phone call from a publicist whom journalists characterize as "spin doctors" would have been ignored. Not only did John take my call but he offered to meet me for lunch at Ollie's Szechuan Restaurant on West 42d St. We talked for nearly an hour. And when it was time to pay the bill, he insisted.

What is remarkable is that the man with whom I was breaking bread was not only generous and a good listener, the former managing editor of *The Times* called him "the most original stylist I'd ever edited."

John stood out in other ways, too. He was about 6 feet 5 inches tall and often described as a latter-day Ichabod Crane. His editors called him "the man of the awkward gait and the graceful phrase." A King James Bible sat on the edge of his desk.

I learned about John after reading *The Kingdom and the Power* by Gay Talese, the epic about *The New York Times*. Phillips was on assignment one day interviewing a man who was a ranking official of the American Nazi Party.

He asked Daniel Burros to confirm that he was raised as a Jew. When Burros digested that, he threatened to kill Phillips if the revelation made the paper. The story ran and upon reading it, Burros shot himself to death.

John and I met on many occasions and the subject was always the same: the newspaper business and how I could best reenter the 4th Estate. John told me he was planning to retire from *The Times* and was looking into the possibility of starting a newspaper that focused entirely on *Good News*. He believed his idea was viable. But that was not to be.

Instead, he continued preaching what John called the Good News. And he did it in the shadow of his rent subsidized apartment off the Columbia University campus while managing the affairs of his New Testament Fellowship congregation.

John came to know Jesus as a young man. I grew up as an Orthodox Jew. Yet we found our faiths bound us together.

Neither John nor I imposed our values on the other. From our similarities a long friendship developed. He came to Philadelphia in 1975 to speak at our congregation. I met his colleagues, some of the top writers and editors at *The Times*. All were well educated and respected journalists. Remarkably, all were devout Christian believers. Among them was Nathaniel Nash, the Frankfurt Bureau Chief of *The Times*. Nathaniel was later killed when the airplane carrying Secretary of Commerce Ronald Brown crashed into a Croatian mountain.

One day John gave me a copy of his book *The Bible, the Supernatural and the Jews*. He signed it, "To Ed Eisen. A fellow laborer in the vineyards of ink." He authored a second book, *City Notebook*. It brought together his best pieces on New York life. Inside the cover he wrote: "To Ed Eisen — Who knows what it is to write on deadline, with every millisecond made precious — come back!"

His comment was an expression of John's hope for me that I would return to my first love: print journalism. Eventually I did.

5
Saturdays With Bill

Bill Schwabe is one of the most fascinating people I have ever met. He is neither famous nor infamous. He arrived in this country as a dispossessed Jewish refugee from Hanau, Germany, fleeing from the Holocaust.

I am awed when I look at the totality of his life: from a dishwasher to Director of Human Resources at Johns Hopkins Hospital, one of America's top medical institutions.

Now at 95, Bill is retired, a widower with only a son who works 900 miles away in the television industry. Bill lives in a personal care community near Philadelphia, assisted round-the-clock by a Russian-speaking aide.

A serious leg injury years ago impaired his mobility and in recent years diminished his independence even more. Sometimes there are senior moments. But overall, Bill continues to be a stickler for detail and punctuality. He follows up on commitments. He expresses his thoughts articulately. His greetings are warm, a broad smile always there, almost as if pasted in position. Surely a good bargaining chip for anyone in labor negotiations. The German accent is ever present. And when he asks, "How are you?" Bill Schwabe really wants to know.

Bill was 17 when he arrived at Ellis Island with his parents and a sister. He labored in a succession of low-end jobs, served in World War II, received a degree from the University of Pennsylvania, worked as a Classifications Officer for Philadelphia and in 1991 authored a memoir, *A Journey Through Separate Worlds*. He wrote in the final paragraph after a revisit to Hanau, the celebrated town of the brothers Grimm: "Hanau felt small and isolated. Somehow the odor of Nazism and Teutonic bombast still wafted through the air. I felt no emotional connection to the town of my birth. I was glad to leave and escape that period of my past."

My wife Marion and I met Bill through an interesting series of coincidences. One of my closest friends at the old *Philadelphia Bulletin* was Gunther David, a German-born newsman who would host New Year's parties at his home in Dresher, a suburb of Philadelphia. Bill lived nearby with his wife Norma. It was at a number of these festive gatherings that we met.

The Schwabes were friendly, congenial but the relationship never took off. It was not until Gunther died and Bill and Norma moved to Rydal Park, an upscale retirement community in Jenkintown, that Marion and I rediscovered them at a wine and cheese tasting reception.

And it was not until Norma died suddenly that Bill and I established a relationship that has lasted for years. Bill is 15 years my senior and some ask: "So Ed, what is it that you guys have in common? What would prompt you to spend two hours with an old man every Saturday?"

Perhaps Bill himself wrestled with the same question when he announced on several visits: "Now, Ed, I want you to know that when I pass, all of my assets go to my son, Andy."

I've always taken the comment as a personal affront. I appreciated my friend's candor but I felt the admonition questioned my motives. I recently expressed to him why Saturdays with Bill carries such special significance.

At the dawn of the 20th century my mother came here with virtually no background on her Jewish heritage. Through me she met Esther Siris, an elderly European immigrant with an extensive knowledge of Jewish culture and tradition.

Every Saturday mom would visit Mrs. Siris. Only illness kept her away. Esther taught mom everything she knew about keeping a kosher home. The visits continued for many years until Mrs. Siris' passing.

Like Esther, Bill has always enjoyed, anticipated my Saturday visits. If I didn't show, there would be a reminder call. "Are you coming today, Ed? We've got a lot to talk about." I'd say: "Could we make it Sunday, Bill?"

Most of Bill's friends have passed. What remains today, he says, are "acquaintances." Over the years Bill has become my mentor, advisor, and confidant. Today I work as a motivational speaker and Bill is my *practice audience*. He has been an honest critic and an invaluable source of inspiration. And when my speechifying hobbles off message, his eyes will close, he'll reflect slowly and gently set me back on track. Everyone needs a friend like Bill Schwabe.

6
Gone Girl

I remember the time my Cousin Joanie, my Uncle Sam and Aunt Edna would ply a darkened stairway to reach my family's 9th floor apartment in Brooklyn. An unmistakable aroma would trail each visit. Uncle Sam would parade through the door with his family cradling a smorgasbord of fresh-cut bagels, salami, pastrami, corned beef, blintzes, knishes and more. The delicacies were his signature love offering from a string of diners he owned and managed over the years. "Okay, everybody," he would bark with that unmistakable accent, a unique blend of Jewish and Cuban. "Settle down, let's eat!"

Back in the mid-30s when Uncle Sam arrived at Ellis Island his vessel was denied entry. He wound up living in Cuba for several years, arriving here with two newly acquired skills. He learned to speak Spanish and became an expert short-order cook. He met my Aunt Edna, my mom's middle sister. The Tischers married and had an only child, my Cousin Joanie. The rest — as they say — is history.

As a little girl Joanie's big pastime was playing make-believe hospital. She would tote a small, black bag into our apartment each week. From inside emerged a toy stethoscope, thermometer, Band-Aids and rolls of Lifesavers. "Are you running a fever?" she would begin with an examination of my ears.

Joanie always managed to uncover some dreaded illness. Then, she'd giggle and a smile would tumble from the pursed lips. "Here, have a Lifesaver," she would chirp. I came to believe my cousin was headed for a career as an actress or a nurse. Joanie was my first love.

She grew into a glamorous teen and almost always there was Shana, a white poodle yapping at her heels. She would regale my Cousin Dick Babush and me with tales about her famous voice coach Carlo Menotti and plans for her career as an opera singer.

We came to see the Tischers less frequently when my family moved to South Jersey and my father found work with an office cleaning company. For many years my Cousin Dick, and his mom, my Aunt May, lived nearby. There was this unspoken rivalry between Dick and me over whose place Joanie would spend the night when her family took the 89-mile trek by car from New York.

Of the three sisters Aunt Edna was the most openly romantic. As the family gathered to feast on Uncle Sam's smorgasbord, she would climb atop his lap to share a pastrami sandwich. But Joanie, as she grew into her teens, became more icy, often twisting her father's name into mocking derision.

One day I took Joanie on a spin around the Airport Circle in a station wagon loaded with my father's work equipment. The black van toppled on its side. No one was injured but the humiliation of that moment lingers to this day.

When Joanie was 18, on one of our extended strolls through the neighborhood, she confided that her voice coach was developing her into a future Maria Callas. "Do you think I have the stuff?" she asked. "I'm in no position to judge," I told her. "I played second fiddle in Camden High School's orchestra. My performance was so poor I was invited to leave."

What came next was some jumbled talk that left me so utterly alarmed that I could barely recognize the attractive young woman crossing Baird Blvd. with me. I listened too embarrassed to ply my cousin with questions. Thirty-five years later the riddle was solved.

7
Girl Found

I was 23 when Marion and I married at a synagogue in Germantown. Among the guests was my cousin Joanie. She arrived late, unaccompanied by her parents. The picture in our wedding album says it all: Cousin Joanie had grown into a stunning, svelte beauty, with movie-star good looks.

The last time I saw Joanie was at my mother's funeral in 1973 when Marion and I lived in Philadelphia. I blurted out something that so enraged my Uncle Sam that he snatched his family and fled from our home. I announced that Marion and I had become Messianic Jews, Jews who believe in Jesus. I explained that we considered ourselves not converted but completed. My beloved uncle was a non-observant Jew who rarely set foot in a synagogue and worked Saturdays. "I'll never come back here again," he barked, hurriedly racing to his car. Aunt Edna and Joanie followed in stunned silence.

Marion and I ran to the car with them. "Get away from me!" he yelled. "You're a traitor. I'll never see you again." The

Cadillac sped off. True to his word, we never saw the Tischer family again.

Years later on a business trip to New York, I called Joanie. She was living in Queens with her mother. Suddenly my cousin's manner turned icy. I could barely discern her mumbling. I asked questions. She provided no answers. After a few minutes the phone clicked. She hung up. Dick, now married and a CPA living in Atlanta, experienced the same behavior when he called.

"Where's Joanie?" we would ask one another over the years.

Once Uncle Sam vowed that upon retirement he and his family would move to Israel where his sister lived. On a visit there in the 80s, Marion and I tried to locate the Tischers in Natanya, a retail diamond community in which I believed they had moved.

I was unsuccessful. Years later, I received a dismaying call from Dick. He told me that, indeed, the family had moved to Natanya. Joanie was committed to a mental institution with a diagnosis of schizophrenia. Sadly, she died there.

There's a footnote to the story. Before Uncle Sam passed, he bought a condo for Joanie, hoping someday she would recover. The apartment had been sitting vacant for years. The taxing authorities wanted their money.

It turns out Uncle Sam's sister had a daughter, a daughter Dick and I never knew existed. Sheila, our family's fourth cousin, lives in Lake Worth, FL. Uncle Sam's will required her to determine if there were any other survivors. Turns out, an elderly cousin turned up. Shelia found Dick. Dick called me.

Now the condo will be sold. Back taxes will be paid. But neither Dick nor I are celebrating our *good* fortune. Our cousin is gone and we'd rather have our Joanie back.

8
Costly Transformation

The departure of my Uncle Sam and his family prompted many to ask *why*. The decision by Marion and me to join a congregation of believers who had found the Jewish Messiah dismayed more than merely my beloved Uncle Sam. Over the years we lost friends, some of whom were close. Our beliefs often left our four children confused.

I grew up in a strictly Orthodox home. My mother served only kosher food. I attended an Orthodox synagogue, studied the Hebrew Bible and Talmudic commentaries. At 13, I was a Bar Mitzvah and wore phylacteries (small leather boxes containing sacred texts worn by observant Jews).

From the very beginning I had an insatiable curiosity that ultimately put me at odds with my family. I remember asking my pop on Yom Kippur, the holiest day of the Jewish year: "Where is God, Pop? He pointed to the second floor of the old Sons of Israel Synagogue in Camden. "See that opening in the door? See the sky? That is where God lives, son," he said.

Coming home from school one day, I was accosted by a group of kids as I was crossing a Catholic school playground. One pony-tailed girl chased after me: "Dirty Jew," she howled, pummeling me to the ground. How she discerned that I was from the tribe of Abraham still puzzles me. My nose — to this day — presents no curves.

"Who is this Jesus?" I remember asking pop soon after that bloody confrontation. "He was a good Jewish man," pop told me. "But many Christians say he was God. Jewish people don't believe that."

My curiosity over the years took me to a Lutheran pastor who tutored me on what the Old and New Testaments had to say about Jesus. I found the account puzzling and after a few weeks quit. Years earlier as a newly enlisted GI aboard a ship enroute to Germany, I met three recruits.

Each was toting a bible. The notion of a baby born of a virgin who turned out to be God failed to meet the credibility test for a newsman, a skeptic the likes of me.

Years later I met Marion, the girl who would become my wife over the next 60 years. She was five years my junior. Her family attended a conservative synagogue in Philadelphia. Soon after we married, Marion and I moved to Florida in a quest to establish a foothold in a career as a journalist and broadcaster. Questions about the real Jewish Messiah continued to evade, and yes, haunt us.

Encyclopedias at libraries offered scant information. Rabbis with whom we met offered grave doubts about New Testament accounts and Gentile interpretations of prophecies found in the Jewish Scriptures. Sadly, these explanations left us only with more questions. Finally, our search took us to Gerald Stanton. Dr. Stanton was a Bible scholar and author who invited Marion and me to his home in Boca Raton in 1963.

He led us to a long series of prophecies found in the Hebrew scriptures (Isaiah 53) about the man whose preaching turned the Roman world of his day upside down. The prophets foretold the story of his birth, death and resurrection nearly 800 years before the events took place. The Christian Bible confirmed the prophesies.

Marion was moved, convinced that Jesus was, indeed, the Messiah. She wept at the discovery. Six months later, my knees trembling, I walked down the aisle of a non-denominational church near Ft. Lauderdale to surrender my life to the man who healed the sick, cured lepers and transformed lives. Years later when Marion and I moved back to Philadelphia we discovered thousands of people just like us — born of Jewish parents — who also believed. On her deathbed I remember the words of my mother when I invoked the name of Jesus: "Get away from me!" she sobbed in Jewish.

Today we are part of a group numbering in the tens of thousands worldwide called Messianic Jews. Back in the mid-90s Marion was led to witness to immigrants whom she discovered on the streets of Northeast Philadelphia. She founded one of the city's first Messianic fellowships for Russians. There she established a free ESL school that operates to this day. And at one point I created a Russian Jobs Network designed to aid these new Americans to find employment here.

9
My Mishpocha

Mishpocha — in Jewish — means The Family. This is not to be confused with the Cosa Nostra. That's Italian, literally meaning Our Affair. More simply put: the Mafia. While it's true — as you'll read in Chapter 12 — the Philadelphia Mafia made me an offer I did refuse. But let it be known that as for the Eisen clan, we never became enmeshed in any underworld criminal activities. You'll just have to take my word for it.

Marion was a steadfast homemaker. She was the one who maintained a showplace home, kept us in clean clothes, plied our bellies with nutritious meals and ensured on-time departure and arrivals for all of us. One exception: I'll never forget the afternoon I came home to find all five encamped around the kitchen table grinning, biting glutinously into a big box of Dunkin' Donuts.

Marion was a gentle task master, tactful advisor, enforcer, encourager. She was wife, mother, nurse, therapist. Bottom line: we all grew up to be outstanding citizens. No mass murderers, no bank robbers, no illegal drug convictions. Like mom and dad all four kids blossomed into well-adjusted adults. All carrot-tops with a dash of freckles sprinkled here and there.

Unlike today's generation of young people, our children did not grow up with any sense of entitlement. With no prompting, they pitched in to help in the kitchen with no expectation of rewards. Perhaps it was understanding the limits of a newspaper man's income, each worked or received grants for scholarships. Came birthdays and anniversaries, the kids remembered mom and dad, often serving breakfast in bed.

Gwen, our first born, was serious minded, humble, obedient to a fault, generous with her time. Eleven years older than her baby sister, she cared for Stacy like a mother. Early on Gwen was moved by those in poverty, those who arrived at her school without pretty dresses, often without breakfast. Gwen went on to receive a master's degree in Social Work and Family Therapy.

Today she labors in some of Philadelphia's most poverty-stricken areas. She is married to an Orthodox Jew. They have four grown children, two living abroad near Jerusalem.

I have concluded Stacy, our youngest child, emerged from the womb with extravagant tastes. Her suburban home is a showplace of modern decor and the aroma of fresh-cut flowers is everywhere.

On a trip to Israel when she was 14, a young South African boy, was smitten by her. Later he traveled to America and stayed at our home for a week. I think Bradley was hoping the relationship would blossom into something permanent. That was not to be. Stacy didn't share his aspirations. Instead — like her mom — Stacy acquired a love affair for other things. For example, shopping malls and baubles. At 16, she worked after school in a jewelry shop. At 18, she enrolled in a community college to study physical therapy. Today her income far outpaces her old man's best earnings. Working from home she is a recruitment specialist in the healthcare industry. Stacy is married to an advertising executive. They have a lovely young daughter. Yes, she too, is a carrot top.

Our two sons — it has been said — possess a creative bent like their dad. At 9, we'd find Seth, our youngest son, attired in black cape and hat waving a magic wand. Youngsters would stream into our garage to witness *The Great Sebastian*. Entrance fee: 10 cents.

We recognized Seth's artistic potential when we found on his desk an incredible pencil likeness to English actor John Gielgud. The sketch, now framed, hangs along with his other works in our Jenkintown apartment. In high school Seth's art teacher was so taken by his student's potential that he gifted him with a key to his studio. Seth was overcome with gratitude. The windfall was a pass to skip gym.

He holds degrees in fine arts, dance and theatre. Seth has taught for many years supporting himself as a working artist.

Stephen, our older son, was a high achiever in elementary and high school where he served as president of the student body. I remember the outdoor market of found objects he assembled on our front lawn one weekend. The purpose: a huge fund raiser for Multiple Sclerosis that drew scores of neighbors from the community.

At his high school Steve played a leading role in *Oklahoma* and graduated at the top of his class. With scholarships and after-school work, he earned a degree in Film and TV from Temple University. He went on to become a top seller for Harper-Collins. Later he established *BE Pictures*, an educational TV production company based in San Francisco. Just as the new business was heating up, Stephen was diagnosed with melanoma. He died at 33.

People ask about how our faith affected our children. Yes, they found confusion in attempting to live as both Christian and Jew. We are deeply saddened by that. "How can you live a life on the fence?" Seth once asked. The Hebrew Scriptures, we told him, speak clearly of the need of the Jewish people for a Messiah. The fulfillment of those prophecies is found in another book written for both Jew and Gentile. It's called the New Testament. At Stephen's passing, he came back to God, again accepting the words found in John 3:16: "Whosoever believes in me shall not perish but have everlasting life."

World-boxing champ Joe Frazier gifts me with the glove that cost him his bout with George Foreman in 1973. (Photo courtesy Gray & Rogers)

NATIONAL CATHOLIC REPORTER

30 minutes with Mother Teresa changed me

Mother Teresa is pictured in a 1979 photo. (CNS/KNA)
Edward N. Eisen | Aug. 26, 201

It was April 1975. The diminutive figure in the white and blue sari was bent and fragile, yet the hand extended was firm and warm. The private meeting on the upper floors of the Philadelphia archdiocese will be forever etched in my memory. Mother Teresa, the beloved Catholic nun from the streets of Calcutta, was having lunch with this Jewish kid from Brooklyn, N.Y.

What an improbable union, a rare moment, a flash in my life that lasted but 30 minutes but dramatically changed me from the inside out.

Mother Teresa pictured in my Op-Ed about our meeting that changed the direction of my career. (Reprinted with permission of *The National Catholic Reporter*)

FRONT ROW SEAT

PROFILE

P.R. Man for Two Popes:
Ed Eisen Stands Alone

BY DAVID MOORE

The editorial offices of *SEP* have set up elaborate safeguards to hold at bay the importunities of P.R. folk. Initial callers are vetted through voice mail. Those circumventing this checkpoint get passed on to a managing editor who runs the show from a bunker of reinforced concrete, 30 floors beneath the earth's surface. She wields her invective to such shocking effect that it's shorted out three censor devices installed on her phone. Only one man could slip through this high-tech fortress.

THIS STORY wasn't supposed to be written. Or, maybe the story was scripted from the start and I just didn't—couldn't—know it.

I was close to assigning a story on the subject of media relations to a man who built a 30-plus year career becoming an expert on the subject. As we went back and forth over specific coverage, something began to gnaw at me. I fought its power as best as I could

Ed Eisen reads national magazines on the Radio Information Service for the blind.

but, in the end, gave in to its inescapable rightness. The writer himself was the story.

Like a jazz riff, Ed Eisen's long career in journalism and media relations is remarkable for the continuities running beneath improvisation. He started off in the 1950s spinning Patti Page and Teresa Brewer songs for

top-40 radio. The 1960s found him hosting talk radio, producing television news and editing *The Fort Lauderdale News*. In 1966, he went to work as a reporter for *The Philadelphia Inquirer* and garnered several awards covering the gritty underbelly of American culture. In 1968, during a wave of terrorist fright, Eisen won a Philadelphia Press Association award by planting a phony bomb in a government building to expose its poor security.

Cover story about history's first Jew representing two popes. (Reprinted with permission of *Self-Employed Professional*)

New York Times journalist John McCandlish Phillips, my friend and mentor. (Photo courtesy of John Orris, *The New York Times*)

Philadelphia Inquirer reporter Ed Eisen posing as a terrorist. (Reprinted with permission of *The Philadelphia Inquirer*)

The Eisen family. Top left: Son Seth, me, daughter Gwen, bottom left: wife Marion, daughter Stacy. (Photo courtesy Seth Eisen)

Our son Stephen who died of melanoma at 33.
(Photographer unknown)

Bill and Lillian Eisen on their wedding day, 1934. (Photographer unknown)

Part 2
The Harvest

10
Pope's Jewish PR Guy

A few years after I left *The Philadelphia Inquirer*, I was hired by one of the city's largest advertising and public relations firms. One day the boss called me into his office at Gray & Rogers to announce that the company was selected to represent Pope Paul VI for an event called The 41st International Eucharistic Congress.

It marked the first time in 50 years the prestigious spiritual assembly would meet in the United States. Philadelphia was selected as the venue, the same city hosting the Bicentennial in 1976. The Congress would draw such luminaries as President Gerald Ford, Mother Teresa, Princess Grace Kelly of Monaco and some of the church's most outspoken critics of Communism. And, of course, the Pope.

I was stunned when the vice president of public relations at the agency asked me to become the point man to handle world-wide publicity for the event. "But, I'm Jewish," I told

Dave Ferrell. "I've never been to Mass, never sat in a Confessional, never attended an infant baptism."

"Don't worry," he said. "You'll learn. You won't have to kiss the Pope's ring. I'll do that next week in Rome. You just handle the news media from Philadelphia."

He told me the selection decision was based on two reasons: One, there was the symbolism: The founder of the Roman Catholic Church was the son of a Jewish carpenter. I would become the first person of the Jewish tradition to serve as spokesman for a pope. A second factor was my experience as a veteran newsman and broadcaster. "Give me a day to think about it," I told Dave.

I stopped by my dad's apartment to seek counsel on what many in Judaism would consider an assignment that crossed the line. Pop had just gone to bed, home from a night of work cleaning offices all over the city. He had been a widower four years. I hesitated to awaken him. During the week he put in a 60-hour work schedule. On weekends, he served as a cantor in synagogues all over West Philadelphia. Funeral directors would call on him to sit with the recently departed, an Orthodox tradition, designed to "keep the devil" from inhabiting the souls of those awaiting burial.

Bleary eyed, pop looked at me with disbelief when I told him what Gray & Rogers was asking. "Eddie," he said, with that unmistakable Eastern European accent. "You had a bris (circumcision), a Bar Mitzvah, you went to Sunday school to learn Hebrew. What do you know about Jesus?"

Then he paused, reflecting on his own experience over a half century earlier. Pop remembered the runaway kid eating from trash cans, sleeping in doorways. He remembered the Roman Catholic priest standing outside St. Cecelia's in Detroit. The pastor beckoned him over. "Are you hungry, young man?" he asked. "Would you like a hot bowl of soup, a warm bed to sleep tonight?" Pop never forgot that kindness. And so, before he closed his eyes again, a smile creased the wrinkled brow. I was startled to hear Pop echo the words of my Roman Catholic boss: "It could be a learning experience."

So the next day I was back at work preparing for the onslaught of a million pilgrims who would be in the city a year later to greet Pope Paul VI. Too ill to travel, the Italian pope never made it. In his place came the man who would serve as Papal Legate and would later be named Pope John Paul II. The experience turned out to be the most unique assignment of my 52 years on the road.

11

Chicken Soup With Mother Teresa

The tiny figure in the white and blue sari was bent and fragile. Yet the hand extended was firm and warm, the smile angelic.

The meeting on the upper floors of the Archdiocese of Philadelphia is etched forever in my memory: The son of an Orthodox Jew sharing a bowl of steaming chicken soup with Mother Teresa, the beloved Catholic nun from the streets of Calcutta.

That union was, indeed, improbable, but true: a brief flash in my life that lasted less than an hour but dramatically transformed me from the inside out.

I was there for an interview that would be dispatched around the world in six languages. I remember the first words the founder of the Missionaries of Charity spoke as she entered the room: "We of the Catholic tradition are so grateful to our

Jewish brothers and sisters. The founder of our faith was also Jewish. As Christians we will always be indebted to you."

It was a life-defining moment to hear the nun who had dedicated her life to the sick and dying speak so. And for a moment, I imagined a halo encircling the sun-furrowed face. She shared with me her work, a work that had established 700 missions in 130 countries around the world.

Before her arrival at our meeting, Mother Teresa had visited Philadelphia's center-city area near the Reading Terminal. She observed on this chilly March day, dozens of homeless men and women huddled in blankets, some sleeping, others begging. The scene prompted the Saint of the Gutters to tell me: "There are thousands of people in Philadelphia who are forgotten, unwanted, hungry for love. We pass them by. Love them. Loneliness is the greatest poverty." Before we parted, Mother Teresa asked how she could *pray* for me.

I told her that my move from journalism to public relations had been a mistake, a disappointment and that crossing back into journalism would be challenging, if not impossible. "Nothing is impossible for God," she said, a smile radiating from her face.

Then, the nun who would be canonized in 2016, offered the best counsel I had ever received in my long career in communications. The Nobel Prize recipient said: "You need not be a nun to have a purpose. But without a mission, life can be very empty. What's your purpose?"

The meeting prompted me to reexamine my *purpose*. Somewhere along my circuitous career path I recognized that it had been lost. Two years later a door that had been shut suddenly opened. I was hired as a business writer at *The Philadelphia Bulletin*.

12

The Mafia and Me

One of the oddest calls I ever received came not in my newspaper career but after I opened Eisen & Associates, an independently-operated public relations firm. The caller identified himself as Ralph Mortorano, the ring leader of the Philadelphia Mafia.

Mortorano was calling from the city's Detention Center, serving 17 years on drug trafficking and murder charges. "Long John" as he was called, asked me to represent his son who had written a manuscript on life in the mob. George — just named *Prisoner of the Year* — had been convicted of running a $75 million a year organized crime drug empire. Now here was his father offering me a contract to help get his kid's work transformed into a Hollywood motion picture.

"Wait a minute," I said. "Out of all the public relations firms in the Yellow Pages, how did you come to call me?" His sister, Mortorano said, delivered an article with a headline that read:

Ed Eisen Stands Alone. PR Man For Two Popes. Mortorano asked me to visit him and George at the prison.

"Are you a religious man?" the head of the Philadelphia Mafia asked. I was taken aback by the question. I told him my father was an Orthodox Jew "My son was an alter boy," came the response.

Then Mortorano was back to business. "Would you come out to meet George? He's a fine writer. Take a look at his manuscript." I declined. Mortorano pressed on: "Well, would you meet with my consigliere? He'll make you an offer you won't be able to refuse."

Something told me the conversation was heading in the wrong direction. Yet — out of curiosity — I met Mortorano's attorney at Dave & Busters at Penn's Landing a few days later. The attorney offered me a $48,000 contract to take George's *Life Inside the Mafia* to Hollywood.

When I arrived home I called an old FBI contact. "Is this legal?" I asked. The agent assured me that even the Mafia had the right to retain PR counsel, just as they would an attorney.

I checked in with my wife. "Are you crazy?" Marion shrieked. "What happens if the Mafia doesn't like your work? Some say Jimmy Hoffa wound up in the Hudson. You could wind up in the Delaware," she warned. Her parting shot: "You're trying to start a new business. I can just picture the headline in the paper: *Ex-Inquirer Reporter Signs Deal With Mafia.*

So the oddest phone call of my career ended as it began with a phone call. "No deal," I told the consigliere.

Ralph was gunned down and killed just outside Thomas Jefferson University Hospital in 2002. George was released 32 years later, holding the record as the longest incarcerated non-violent offender in the federal prison system. He authored several books and helped educate and rehabilitate hundreds of inmates.

13

The Millionaire

It began with a phone call from an ex-Marine who was now earning a living as a matchmaker for the Main Line wealthy. Would I have an interest in playing a role in the biggest manhunt since famed aviator Charles Lindberg received a ransom note demanding $50,000 for the return of his infant son? That's how the conversation began.

I had been referred by a former *Philadelphia Inquirer* colleague. At that time in my career, I had left the newspaper business and was working as a public relations consultant. "I'm a publicist, not a private eye," I told Allen Miller. "That's what Bipin Shah is looking for," Miller told me. "Private eyes have turned up zilch," he cackled.

"Who's Bipin Shah?" I asked. Bipin Shah, Miller told me, was the self-made Philadelphia Main Line millionaire banker, architect of the ATM machine.

"But why would Bipin Shah need a PR guy?" I pressed on.

Shah's two daughters, Sarah, 8 and Genevieve, 6 went missing three months earlier with their mother, Ellen Dever Shah. Vanished into what Shah would later tell me was an organization known as the *Children of the Underground,* a network run from a Dunkin' Donut shop in Atlanta by self-appointed vigilante Faye Yager. This coal miner's daughter, wife of a physician, helped men and women flee with their kids to escape partners alleged to have been abusive. Usually courts had granted custody to both parents.

Shah hired private investigators on four continents, attracted some 100 bounty hunters and turned his suburban mansion into an international command center. The search dragged on for months with no success.

Later, sitting in his home, Shah told me that publicity was the missing element required to ferret out the location of his girls. We agreed to a $10,000 monthly retainer.

I assured him all we needed for success was a sizable award offered to bounty hunters that would lead to information on where his family was hiding. I suggested a $1 million reward, a sum that would well exceed the $50,000 Lindberg offered in 1932 for his missing son. Shah upped the bounty to $2 million.

With that I went to work. I checked in with newspapers in Philadelphia, New York, London, around the world. In a couple months I returned with a one- paragraph story that appeared in *USA Today.* Shah was not happy. He cut my retainer to $5,000 monthly.

I learned from the National Center for Missing and Exploited Children why the story was failing to attract interest. In

1996 there were more than 350,000 intra-family abductions in the U.S. each year, nearly 1,000 daily. Almost half —163,000 — involved concealment of the child, transporting out of state or intent to keep the child permanently.

Suddenly, I was struck by an ah-ha moment. I had come to know Steve Lopez, a *Philadelphia Inquirer* columnist who had moved on as a staff writer for *TIME Magazine*. (Lopez later authored *The Soloist* that would become a major Hollywood hit.)

I convinced Lopez to visit Shah with me at his home. He caught the drama I envisioned from the beginning. What followed was *Hide and Seek,* a cover story in *Time* on May 11, 1998. The cover depicted Shah, sad, forlorn, cradling a rag doll. In the background were images of Sarah and Vivi.

The rest — as they say — is history. The news media around the world jumped on the story. So nearly two years after the manhunt began, the girls and their mom were recovered walking on a quiet street in Luzerne, Switzerland.

Shah spent $3.2 million of his fortune to find his kids, now in their late 20s. None of his fortune went to the bounty hunters whose leads turned out to be worthless.

14

Joe Frazier's Glove

One of my clients at Gray & Rogers was Germantown Savings Bank (GSB), a regional Goliath that had just acquired a new-fangled technology akin to today's smart phones. They called it *Pay-by-Phone*. Customers could pay a bill by picking up a phone and punching in a series of numbers. Waiting in line at the utility company to pay a bill or spending what was then 13-cents for a postage stamp was suddenly old school.

A customer could dial GSB, enter a code and follow a series of phone prompts. And all this for just 10-cents. So GSB became Philadelphia's first "high-tech" bank to offer the service. Pay-by-Phone opened the door to a market with tens of thousands of potentially new customers. There was but one problem: how to sell the concept to Philadelphia.

That's how I was transformed overnight in my new career from journalist to Barnum & Bailey show barker. The transition did not come easily. Gray & Rogers — AT&T's ad company — was commissioned with the task of fashioning a campaign that would make Pay-By-Phone as popular as the telephone Alexander Graham Bell invented in 1876.

It was at that point we brainstormed the notion of retaining boxing champ Joe Frazier. The marketing campaign pictured Joe punching out a telephone with Eagles quarterback Bill Bergey. That's the back story of how I came to walk up three flights of steps to Joe's North Philadelphia gym.

The gym served as a training center for Frazier's highest profile bouts against Muhammad Ali and George Foreman. Indeed, he was a slugger who weathered repeated blows to the head while delivering punishment. He won 32 fights in all, 37 by knockouts, losing four times, twice to Muhammad Ali and twice to Foreman.

In 1973 he was defeated by Foreman in a 2.5 round technical knock-out. I found him in the ring coaching a promising 19-year old. During a break, I asked: "Joe, how would you like to make a fast five grand? All you'd have to do," I said, "is pose in a couple photos punching out a telephone."

The ex-champ scratched his head. I explained. Then he smiled broadly. "Run it by my agent," he suggested. Two weeks later Joe Frazier strolled into our agency at 1234 Market St. to put Germantown Savings Bank on the map.

After the session, I handed Frazier a Sharpie. He penned these words on the big, red Tuff-Wear glove: "To Ed Eisen … Boogie Boogie. Joe Frazier."

Now after all these years the red glove that cost Frazier his match with Foreman, sits on a shelf in our living room. Perched beside the glove is a framed photo of a younger me and the champ at age 32. Often when I speak to groups, I'll say: "Want to come see *The Glove?* You're all invited for dinner tonight." That usually gets a laugh when my wife chimes in from the audience: "Really? Who's cooking?"

15
A Beautiful Mind

I met John Forbes Nash, Jr., the Princeton University mathematician whose life inspired the film, *A Beautiful Mind*. Some would suggest the Nobel Prize winner was crazy, delusional. Yet I perceived something else when I interviewed him that night at Temple University's Diamond Club.

I sat with Nash and his wife Alicia during an awards ceremony honoring his work. He appeared anything but mad. I was there to write a story about what a true genius might say on the politics of game theory, the study of strategic decision-making using mathematical models. We never got to touch on the subject.

But what we did talk about was Nash's take on *what makes a beautiful mind*. The greatest mathematician of the 20th century told me that "anyone's mind can be beautiful" if one focuses on producing "beautiful ideas." Pale and gaunt, the man who had suffered from a life-long battle with paranoid schizophrenia, tried to muster a smile.

Alicia, sitting beside him, was credited with saving Nash's life after his mental illness derailed his career in the 1960s. She let Nash into her home and looked after him even after they divorced in 1963.

Speaking in muted tones, Nash characterized the award-winning motion picture about his life as an "artistic interpretation that failed to describe accurately the nature of my delusions or treatment." Hardly touching his dinner, Nash complained that "mental illness had an unfavorable course in history in the sense that people never really recover to "what you can call being mentally well."

He pulled his chair from the table, peering at me intently: "They become what are called consumers of mental health organizations. They are always taking some sort of pill."

Despite the challenges Nash faced for so many years of his life, his achievements went on to inspire generations of mathematicians, economists and scientists influenced by his work in game theory.

He credited much of his achievements to his parents and grandparents. "They bought me books and encyclopedias. And that's how I learned," he said.

Sylvia Nasar, Nash's biographer, wrote in her 1998 book, *A Beautiful Mind*, that it was "his genius…to choose a woman who would prove so essential to his survival." That chapter of his relationship with Alicia did not make it into the Hollywood version of their lives in the 2001 Oscar-winning film, *A Beautiful Mind*, starring Russell Crowe and Jennifer Connelly.

I felt such remorse when I learned of the tragic death of John and Alicia on the New Jersey Turnpike in May 2015. The couple were returning from an awards ceremony in Sweden when the taxi in which they were riding went out of control. The Nashes left behind a son, John Charles Nash, who inherited both his father's genius and his mental illness.

16

The Warehouse

Do you remember "Deep Throat?" That was code for the government whistle blower who delivered to *The Washington Post* the information that forced President Nixon out of office in the huge Watergate scandal.

One man stands out as the *deep throat* in my career as a journalist, the secret source of my biggest scoop. It was his phone call one night to *The Philadelphia Inquirer* that set in motion a Page 1 scandal that resulted in the closing of Pennsylvania's worst nightmare.

Now the story can be told. His name was Allen Taub. Days he drove a white truck on the streets of the city hawking cheesecakes to restaurants. Emblazoned on the side of the van were the words, *Linda's Cheesecakes.* His baking company was named for his daughter Linda, blind and intellectually challenged since birth. (Back then that euphemism was not in our vernacular. People were labeled retarded.)

After a few years, the Taubs could no longer care for Linda's needs at home. She was placed, like nearly two thousand others in an early 20th century brick and stone structure in Spring City, Chester County. Its name still runs shudders through my spine: Pennhurst State School and Hospital.

Young children lay in their own excrement for hours each day. Others were chained to cribs or quieted by drugs — some over drugged, kept in round-the-clock, zombie-like states. Strands of sticky paper hung from ceilings to ensnare swarms of horseflies.

Health inspectors reported that the institution was understaffed. Aides had become little more than jailers and their helpless charges inmates. Over the years Pennhurst had deteriorated into a warehouse for the sick, the blind, for those born with illnesses that defied cures.

It was under these bedeviling circumstances that prompted Allen Taub to call me one night at *The Inquirer*. He became the "Deep Throat" that ultimately blew the whistle on Pennhurst. "Please don't mention my name," he whispered. "You've got to go out there and see this snake pit for yourself. Bring a photographer." I did. And what followed was a year-long series that drew community activists to demand that the institution be cleaned up or shut down.

My story was followed by a documentary on WCAU-TV with the late John Facenda and newsman Bill Baldini. It was chronicled, *Suffer the Little Children,* a quote from Jesus in the New Testament imploring the leadership of his day to attend the needs of those unable to speak for themselves.

Yet justice moved slowly for the children of Pennhurst. It took 19 years for the Pennsylvania Legislature under Gov. Raymond Broderick to push through a bill that ultimately closed this 20th Century snake pit. Today every Halloween kids clad as witches and zombies flock to the facility to fill their bags with sweets: a somber reminder of a time Pennsylvania's lawmakers slept.

17

America's Gandhi

I met the Rev. Martin Luther King, Jr. in a basement recreation room at Ebenezer Baptist Church in North Philadelphia.

Sitting silently in the half-lit space with Dr. King were aides Whitney Young and James L. Farmer. The news conference was hastily called. I was there representing *The Philadelphia Inquirer*. *The Philadelphia Bulletin* failed to send a reporter — evidence to some — that the civil rights movement in the country was losing steam. There were also camera crews from two of the three major TV stations.

Dr. King sat there at a long table on this sweltering summer day in 1966 in a church with the same name as the one his grandfather had served in Atlanta. He appeared uncomfortable, stressed, wiping perspiration from his face with a handkerchief. Perhaps it was a combination of the summer humidity and the stress of his brutal life on the road, but I could sense the utter frustration in his remarks: "If we are wrong, the Supreme Court of this nation is wrong. If we are wrong, the Constitution of the

United States is wrong. And if we are wrong, God Almighty is wrong," he told the small gathering.

"If we are wrong, justice is a lie, love has no meaning. And we are determined to work and fight until justice runs down like water, and righteousness like a mighty stream," Dr. King said.

Two years before I met the Nobel Prize recipient, King led a voter registration march from Selma to Montgomery, AL. As police strong-armed and beat protesters, the news media chronicled the event as "bloody Sunday." It was marked by arrests of marchers who were trampled and hosed as they attempted to cross the Edmund Pettus Bridge.

In the late 50s Dr. King led a bus boycott that lasted 382 days. The civil rights leader was arrested more than 20 times and assaulted at least four times. His home was bombed. He was subjected to personal abuse as an African-American leader of the first rank. He showed us pictures of himself in a hospital room, his broken nose decked with bandages.

In the Philadelphia news conference Dr. King expressed concern about the turtle-like movement of Congress to take action on a voting rights bill President Johnson was waiting to sign. The civil rights leader also made headlines over his dismissal of the Vietnam War.

"The war," he said, "was destroying the character of the United States but also the character of its soldiers." He viewed the war as "an enemy of the poor," as young black men were sent to "guarantee liberties in Southeast Asia which they had not found in southwest Georgia and East Harlem."

King argued for an ever-expanding moral solidarity that would include those we think of as the enemy. "Here is the meaning of compassion and nonviolence," he said, "when it helps us to see the enemy's point of view." Meanwhile, FBI Director J. Edgar Hoover was monitoring King's activities, apparently ready to spring into action if protests became too violent, ready to link King's activities to a Cold War Communist plot.

"Our lives begin to end the day we become silent about things that matter," America's Gandhi said. Those were the last words I heard Dr. King speak before he left North Philadelphia that day. Two years later I was saddened to learn of his assassination on the balcony of the Lorraine Motel in Memphis.

18

Jackie Gleason's Send-Off

The deal was struck in 1964 over champagne in New York City, sparking what would prove to be a long love affair between Jackie Gleason and South Florida.

And how sw-e-e-t it was! The Maestro of Mirth and his television show entourage gave South Florida six years of showbiz glamour unseen before. *BANG-SIZ ZOOM! Right to the moon!*

That was the time the Great One traded his Manhattan skyline for a tropical tan line. Broward and Palm Beach counties shared in the magic. And I had an opportunity to glimpse some of it, too. But in the end, I stumbled and blew it. Here's what happened:

I was a rookie reporter at an evening paper that no longer exists, *The Fort Lauderdale News*. Those were the days when reporters packed both pad and camera. Gleason, a Brooklyn-born high school drop-out, was rehearsing for his radio show. I was assigned to grab a picture and write a story.

I was excited about working on the Gleason feature because millions tuned in around the country to hear the famous introduction: *From the fun and Sun Capital of the World, Miami Beach, it's the Jackie Gleason Show!*

The deal that pumped life into Miami Beach's tourism industry was hatched in Palm Beach County at the glamorous Biltmore Hotel right where I was heading in my 1956 Ford Fairlane.

Gleason had visited Lantana — five minutes from where I lived — on an invitation from some golfing buddies. He liked Florida enough to do several segments of his short-lived radio show from the hotel.

He was enamored with living in South Florida and playing golf every day. But when he signed on with CBS to broadcast weekly he said he would do business only with the mayor. Mayor Melvin Richard flew to New York to negotiate the deal.

Richard remembered that Gleason wanted to know what he wanted to drink and his golf handicap. Within four hours, Gleason wrapped up the details -- and several bottles of champagne. The city agreed to spend $250,000 to refurbish the Miami Beach Auditorium. Gleason put in another $300,000 and promised to plug the resort during each show.

I had already cleared the interview with Gleason's staff and presented my press credentials when I arrived at the hotel. I walked behind the ballroom stage and found Gleason in rehearsal with Audrey Meadows and several other actors. Here was my moment: My *Front Row Seat* with a guy so famous that many remember his *Honeymooners* episodes even today as the blundering bus driver Ralph Kramden jousting with his neighbor Ed Norton (Art Carney). The duo became one of television's first great comedy teams.

    I sat, observing and waiting. During a break in the rehearsal I was introduced. I told Gleason that I wanted to start with a good action shot. I loaded my Yashica 44 with a flash bulb. The flash didn't go off. I inserted another bulb. Nothing happened. I tried again, beads of sweat sprouting from my forehead.

    The Great One's face turned red. "Get outa here!" he yelled, his voice booming into the empty ballroom. "What's a matter? Can't your paper give you a camera that works?"

    I left the stage humiliated. In all my years as a journalist this incident will remain as *my most embarrassing moment*. I returned to *The Ft. Lauderdale News* with neither picture nor story.

19

Lion of the Senate

When you think of Ted Kennedy what comes to mind? Do you think of the Massachusetts senator as one of the longest serving in U.S. history? *The Lion of the Senate?* After all, until his passing in 2009, he was re-elected nine times, holding the seat 46 years. Or do you remember Ted Kennedy for his civil rights record, his support of America's poor, for championing universal health care?

Or do you remember the youngest of the Kennedy brothers emerging from a car in Plymouth, PA, a white neck brace framing a grimaced countenance? He opened the door for his wife, Joan, soon to undergo her third miscarriage. The couple were to follow the throng into St. Vincent's Roman Catholic Church. I was there as a reporter with *The Philadelphia Inquirer.*

The event was the funeral of Mary Jo Kopechne, the young woman who suffocated and died in Kennedy's black Oldsmobile sedan on the night of July 18, 1969, an event some say that led to the fall of the House of Kennedy. The facts, literally etched in the American psyche, are these: The 37-year-old senator left a party near Martha's Vineyard with Mary Jo when his car went off a bridge, landing upside down on Chappaquiddick Island.

Kennedy swam to safety but his late brother's aide, Mary Jo, died in the overturned vehicle. Kennedy fled the scene and failed to report the accident for nearly 10 hours. Following an investigation, he was given a suspended sentence for leaving the scene. The exact details of what happened that night remain murky even to this day.

Kennedy delivered a brief televised speech on July 25, 1969, saying there was no reason to suspect him of immoral conduct. Mary Jo, he said, was known as a young woman of impeccable character. The events of that evening, he reported, were cloudy but he claimed he made specific efforts to save Kopechne.

He characterized his efforts for failing to call the police immediately as "indefensible." His driver's license was temporarily suspended.

Mary Jo's parents insisted on paying themselves for the cost of the funeral. They received a compensation from Kennedy of $90,000 and another $50,000 in insurance monies. Kennedy announced after the incident that he would not run for the Democratic nomination in the 1972 presidential election. Nor did he run in 1976. But in 1979, he challenged Jimmy Carter for the Democratic Party nomination. Carter selectively referenced the incident at Chappaquiddick, ending for good Kennedy's presidential aspirations.

The Lion of the Senate — as he was sometimes called — died of a brain tumor at age 77, almost 40 years to the day of Mary Jo's funeral in her hometown of Plymouth, PA. Yet there's a personal twist to one of political history's most tragic of all events:

The cover story in the August 1, 1969 issue of *Life Magazine* carries the headline: *The Fateful Turn for Ted Kennedy. Grave questions about his midnight car accident.* Inside is a picture of Kennedy emerging from an automobile wearing a neck brace at the funeral of Mary Jo. He is surrounded by a sea of reporters and photographers. I am standing nearby, a notebook and pen clutched in my left hand. I hollered out, "Why did you take nine hours to report the accident?" There was no response.

20

Hangman's Noose

The four-hour jailhouse interview with Herb F. Steigler at the New Castle County Correctional Institution near Wilmington will always remain etched in my memory.

Did He or Didn't He? That was the headline of the story I penned for *The Philadelphia Inquirer Magazine*. Had I been a member of the jury panel a verdict would not have come easily. Here's what happened:

Steigler, a former Lutheran Sunday school teacher, was convicted and sentenced to hang for setting his house on fire, an inferno that took the life of Chrissy, his six-year old daughter and his wife's parents.

A jury of eight men and four women were convinced Steigler was trying to bail himself out of huge debts with $104,000 in fire and life insurance. The prosecutor characterized Steigler as an adulterer and embezzler. He was sentenced to hang in the state's first execution in 35 years.

My interview took place in the warden's office and then moved to Steigler's jail cell where I saw a picture of a smiling child hanging from the wall.

"Chrissy was my little girl," he said, his voice choking. "The baby of my family. If I did this thing I could not stand to look at her." He peered unflinchingly into my eyes. "I may be guilty of a lot of other crimes. But the crime of setting my house on fire and killing my own flesh and blood and my wife's parents, of that I am innocent," he told me, his voice even, unshaken.

The jury saw Herb Steigler as the man who, on the morning of Oct. 19, 1968, placed 10 plastic, metal and glass containers of gasoline about his Cape Cod home in a Wilmington suburb while his wife and family slept. He repeated over and over, an arsonist set the fire.

On that awful night, Steigler told me as we sat in his jail cell, he scooped up his 11-year-old son David from a first-floor bedroom and ran from the house. Moments later he placed a ladder against the house and rescued his wife from a second-floor bedroom. Another child was sleeping in the home of a girlfriend.

On five occasions, he testified during the trial, he tried to re-enter the burning house. Once Arlene, his wife, restrained him "because she knew that I wouldn't make it out alive," he said.

Steigler sat there gazing at me calmly, his eyes meeting mine, smoke drifting up from his pipe. Then he broke the silence: "Many times I lie on my bunk and I wish Arlene hadn't stopped me. She could have been spared the embarrassment of all this."

Steigler — as we spoke — struck me as a likable, gregarious sort of guy, a giant of a man on a 6-foot-4-inch frame. He told me he was glad I came. Somehow I could not help but believe him.

Steigler's sentence was vacated by the Delaware Supreme Court in 1973 on grounds that evidence was seized without a warrant. He died peacefully 44 years later at a Wilmington nursing home. He was 86.

21

Bag Lady

The sight I saw so many years ago when I worked as a reporter for the old *Philadelphia Bulletin,* is a scene you can spot readily today if you stroll down to the mall near Independence Hall.

She was sitting on a park bench with two shopping bags, her hands pensively folded.

"Hello," I smiled. "Do you have a home?"

"I do. And you're in it. Get the hell out of here!" the woman shrieked, her blue eyes blazing, her cheeks a blotchy red.

Here on this balmy spring-like day sat this figure in the hub of the nation's Cradle of Liberty, a few hundred yards from the Liberty Bell.

She was perhaps in her early 40s, dressed with layer upon layer of clothing. She wore an unbuttoned black raincoat over two sweaters, a blouse, blue runners' pants, and heavy wool socks. Her feet were nestled in ankle-high men's working shoes. Her strawberry-blonde hair was parted and pulled back in a bun.

"Are you hungry? Can I buy you something to eat?" I asked.

The woman rose to her feet, raising her arm: "Get out of here or I'll slam you one!"

I was reminded that day about homelessness by an expert who spoke on Crisis and Suicide Prevention. "We tend to rationalize the problem," said William Eisenhuth. "We pretend it's not here. We make jokes of it. We call them bag ladies, bag men, duck ladies. We rob them of their personhood. But these people have a personhood. These people have a history. Once they were babies in someone's arms."

Lesson learned: the next time I found a homeless person on the street I resisted the temptation to drop a dollar into their plate. I looked for a nearby McDonald's. And I listened to their story.

22

Dating Christine

Some years ago I had a date with famed transsexual Christine Jorgensen. "How would this 37-year old former GI behave if I invite her on a fishing excursion off the Atlantic in Ft. Lauderdale?" I asked my editor at the old *The Ft. Lauderdale News*.

It was a silly idea that no editor would sanction given today's #MeToo Movement and the sexually charged climate in which we live. But back in 1963 Barc Bowman agreed I was onto something to check out how Christine's life had changed when she was transformed from George William Jorgensen, Jr. into a woman.

The son of a carpenter, George grew up in the Bronx. At an early age, he became aware of feeling like a woman stuck inside a man's body. He hated boys' clothes and wondered why his clothes were so different from his older sister Dorothy's pretty dresses.

Jorgensen put his concerns aside when he was drafted into the military in 1945. After being discharged a year later, he floundered for a bit before deciding to become a woman.

In 1950 he traveled to Denmark to begin the transformation. The treatment, available only in Europe at the time, included hormone therapy and several operations. George's story became public in 1952 while he was still in a Copenhagen hospital. So pleased was George with the result, she took the name of her surgeon, Dr. Christian Hambuger.

When she returned to the states Jorgensen became the subject of ridicule. Even the government was not willing to fully recognize her as a female. Engaged, she was denied a marriage license in 1959 because her birth certificate listed her as "male."

Overwhelmed by the attention, Jorgensen had to deal with such headlines as *Bronx 'Boy' Is Now a Girl* and *Dear Mum and Dad, Son Wrote, Have Now Become Your Daughter.*

Christine was performing in a nightclub in Miami Beach when I reached out to her by phone. TV commercials showcased her in Wonder Woman garb singing *I Enjoy Being a Girl.* "Sure, I'll drive out to meet you," she responded to my request for a date.

I helped a smiling Christine board the fishing skiff I had rented. She was blonde, slender, attired in white shorts and sneaks. Christine had made a new life for herself as an entertainer, actress and nightclub singer. She regularly received offers to appear naked.

"Are you happy?" I asked.

"She smiled, her voice still throaty, responding in the affirmative. "I have changed a great deal," Christine smiled, her eyes confirming what she described as her inner joy. "But it's the other changes that are so much more important. I'm no longer the shy, miserable person who left America. That person is no more."

I took a few pictures and we were back at the pier in Ft. Lauderdale in less than an hour. When I returned to the office, my editor cackled: "Well, what happened? Did she pull anything?"

The story I wrote said it all: *Christine's Catch: Three Mackerel.*

23

Feds Flunk Security Test

A bomb went off in a men's room at the United States Capitol some 30 years before the 9/11 attack on our country. No one was killed or injured this time. But clearly the incident caused a lot of panic. A group calling itself the *Weathermen* accepted responsibility for setting off the incendiary device in protest over the Vietnam War.

My editors at *The Philadelphia Inquirer* wondered whether federal buildings in Philadelphia were safe. So on this chilly day on March 4, 1971 I went to check out the Federal Courthouse at 9th and Market Streets. The courthouse was a monster of an edifice containing the U.S. District Court, the Eastern District Third Court of Appeals, dozens of courtrooms and judges' chambers and the U.S. Post Office. Passing the guard station was easy. I offered my press pass. Yet my appearance — one would think — should have cast some suspicion. I was wearing a black Russian headpiece, a grey overcoat and carried a black umbrella. In my left hand I clutched a black briefcase. Inside was a ticking alarm clock. (See Photo, Page 49)

The clock was wrapped in a pair of striped men's shorts, a last-minute ploy designed to muffle the clamor from inside. Yet who could not have missed the sound of the clock? It was clearly audible: *tick-tock, tick-tock, tick-tock.* No one noticed. I sighed a breath of relief and slipped past the security guard free to execute our faux terrorist plot.

There were seven floors in the building. I walked six. Entry to the seventh was locked. The corridors were spotlessly clean. Secretaries greeted me with friendly *hellos.*

Two waved and smiled: "Hello, Commissioner." That was odd. As a reporter I had never been assigned to cover this building. Perhaps a secretary mistook me for someone else.

Over the next 91 minutes I moved from floor to floor. I spent my time in men's rooms mimicking the terrorists in Washington. Except there was no plan to set off a bomb. No suspicions were aroused except once. A man in a pinstriped suit walked in and eyed me with curiosity. He found me scribbling notes onto a pad.

The briefcase with the ticking clock sat resting on the tile floor. Suddenly, I was seized with panic. "Uh-oh," I thought: "The game is up." The man left and minutes later I exited the washroom still undetected. At one point I left my briefcase on a chair in the fourth-floor office of the U.S. Attorney. I returned five minutes later to retrieve it. The secretaries never looked up.

When my inventory of security safety at the Federal Courthouse ended, I exited the building through the U.S. Post Office door on 9th Street. No one questioned me.

The headline in *The Inquirer* the next day read: *Federal Courthouse Flunks Reporter's Security Check.* My hunch is that the story prompted a few changes.

24

Town Going Dry

One of the oddest stories I ever covered didn't take place in Philadelphia but 143 miles away in Greenwich, CT.

The year was 1981 and I was working on a features story for the old *Philadelphia Bulletin*. I hopped an Amtrak to learn that in this majestic town of what was then 60,000 people, something stunk. Yes, I said stunk. Folks were not showering or washing their Bentleys. I could hear the clatter of drillers' rigs on the front lawns of estate homes, in the driveways of carwashes and at the entrance of a community hospital.

In fact, the latest status symbol in Greenwich was to give your wife a well for her birthday. Former New York Mayor Edward Koch joked to a TV interviewer that one could detect residents of Greenwich by their smell.

Residents told me the water company and the politicians were to blame for the town's problems. "You don't have to wait until you have 19 days of water storage to call a water emergency," one lady told me as she prepared for a cocktail party without ice. Meanwhile, it had become common for visitors to bring their hosts 10-gallon jugs of water. Well-drilling was becoming so prevalent that there were two-week waiting lists.

Drillers told me their business was booming at a time when they otherwise would be idled by cold weather. Many townspeople blamed both the water company and politicians for the Greenwich dilemma. Some assailed the utility for permitting unchallenged corporate growth with an antiquated water supply that was working a hardship on long-established residents.

A sign erected on the highway beckoned: *Be a Supersaver! Don't flush. Play poker: five of a kind makes a flush.*

"There's an archaic water system in this town," said one builder. A beauty shop owner agreed. "There are 25,000 people who come into Greenwich every day to go to work. Only 10,000 people are going out. Do you realize how many toilet flushes that amounts to?"

Now 40 years later the town is restricting lawn irrigation. Since 2017 Greenwich mandates when residents and businesses can water their lawns through automatic sprinklers and irrigation systems. The conservation effort has been credited with helping the town's water supply remain strong. Oh, yes, on my last visit things were smelling like roses!

25

Mass Murderer

At 39, Leo Held was a good father, Boy Scout leader, high school board member, an elder in his Christian church. But on this day he came to work angry, *very angry*.

The 6-foot, 200-pounder had become engaged in an altercation with members of his car pool a day earlier. Held also had some issues with supervisors at the old Hammermill Paper plant in Lock Haven, PA where he had worked as a lab technician for 20 years. The pay raises had stopped abruptly and Held came to believe termination was around the bend.

He was a quiet, distinguished looking man. So on this day, Oct. 23, 1967, he arrived at work with two pistols, a rifle and a pocket full of ammo. Held entered the plant in a rampage, shot and killed four members of his car pool, a switchboard operator at the local airport and an elderly man sleeping in his bed. Six others were wounded. Then Held fled in his station wagon to the home of his next-door neighbor, a widow. She was someone he wanted dead. A police sharp shooter took

Held down as he stood knocking on Mrs. Floyd Quiggle's door. Bullets shattered his shoulder, leg and right wrist.

An editor at *The Philadelphia Inquirer* assigned me to piece together the sordid tale. I drove 201 miles to Lock Haven arriving after print and broadcast news journalists had left to file their stories. I found Held alone and semi-conscious in a recovery room at the hospital. A white sheet covered him except for his face. I suspected that a police guard had left on a break. I quietly whisked into his room. Held opened his eyes and whispered what were his last four words: "One more to go."

26

Big Bank, Bad Loans

This is the story of a former Philadelphia Federal Reserve economist who allowed over-confidence to cost him his $216,769-plus a year job at what was once the Goliath of banks in the region.

When I asked John Bunting why First Pennsylvania Corp., a holding company with $9.6 billion in assets, had slipped from a No. 1 ranking to 45, he blamed the recession.

So assured was he of his job, he said he turned down an offer for a prestigious position at an out-of-state university.

"I think Philadelphia needs a philosopher," he told me. "More than one. More than just me," he said in an interview that appeared in a five-part series I wrote for the old *Philadelphia Bulletin*.

But the facts on the table were that First Pennsylvania Corp, with 349 domestic offices in 25 states and 45 foreign countries, *was in trouble.*

Aggressive investments had turned the bank into Philadelphia's largest. But in 1980 huge losses and panicked depositors prompted regulators to put First Pennsylvania on its watch list. Not only that but the U.S. Treasury gave the bank a $500 million bailout, the first major federal bailout of a national bank.

First Pennsylvania, an institution that stood for centuries as the oldest in the United States, was acquired by CoreStates Financial Corporation. John Bunting was asked to resign by his board.

27

Hot TV News

Before the era of action news, rating wars and teleprompters, folks would sit for hours Sunday nights to watch a Temple University speech professor tell them what was happening.

His name was John Roberts and in 1959, the tall, erudite gentleman of mellow voice, urbane wit and the easy adlib taught me about the fickle business of television when I sat in his class as a freshman. He was the dean of Channel 6's *Weekend Report* once vying for viewers with that other John across the street. Yes, that John Facenda on Channel 10.

I was 18 when I first met John Roberts. His gait was ramrod straight and his voice, incredibly sonorous. Roberts had not been performing on TV for 11 years. He had been replaced by a younger face, one of his students. He was considered by industry moguls as a good hit-man in his half-hour weekly public affairs forum that eventually evolved into the station's 15-minute nightly news format. Those were the pre-happy-talk days of television. And Roberts would appear before the cameras armed with a pleasant smile and a bounty of late-breaking news ripped from the station's clatter of non-stop teletype machines.

There was no news film and an occasional still picture. The heat was so intense in the studio "you could see the beads of sweat pouring down my forehead," Roberts told me. For a business with a fickle reputation, he amassed a tenure that spanned 19 years at the station.

When I sat in his class John was performing regularly before another kind of audience, live audiences of hundreds of students like me seeking an entrance into a business almost as impenetrable as copping a role in a Broadway show.

Years later when I interviewed him as a reporter at *The Philadelphia Bulletin,* he was 63 and continued to pack a full house at the school and radio station he founded and directed, Temple's School of Radio, Television and Film, then the country's largest with a class of 1,300.

"Sure, I loved those days at Channel 6," my old professor told me. "But you're not going to find me sitting down and sulking about what was. I'm the kind of person when I finish one phase of my life, I find other exciting things to do."

Roberts' first love since 1946, he told me, was teaching. And when a former student, Charles Burke, replaced him on Channel 6's *Weekend Report* in 1970, Roberts said he could only smile and feel a sense of pride.

I lost touch with my old professor for two decades until one day I wound up sitting at the same table with him when I joined Broadcast Pioneers of Philadelphia, a 500-plus member organization dedicated to collecting and promoting information about the broadcast industry. John was president of the state-chartered club for two years and inducted into its Hall of Fame in 1996. He died at age 94 in a retirement community in Rydal. I never knew that until I read his obituary in *The Inquirer*. It turns out Marion and I live just across the street.

28

Spitballs Flying

If you want to blow your cool, your mind and your voice in six hours flat, try teaching a consolidated 4th grade class of some of the brightest and most backward kids in the Philadelphia school system.

This is what I did one Friday at the J. Hampton Moore Public School in Northeast Philadelphia as striking teachers picketed outside the building across the street from where we lived.

The day wound up with my nine-year-old son, Stephen, telling me he didn't learn a thing in my classroom. That's odd. I learned plenty.

I learned that classrooms manned by parent-volunteers are destined to collapse. At best, parents can be successful babysitters or bullies. But when they come unprepared to teach new math and the three R's in a classroom of mixed learning abilities, they may find themselves in a place well above their experience level.

I stepped out of my house on this Friday morning, walked past the somber-looking pickets and into Moore. I met Principal Isadore Snyderman in the hallway. A worried look creased his tired face. I was on assignment as a reporter with *The Philadelphia Inquirer*.

"Here I am," I announced cheerfully not anticipating what lay ahead. "I'm ready to teach."

"What are your credentials?" he asked pleasantly.

I wanted to tell him that my teaching experience over the past 10 years was limited to potty training three children. My face reddened as the thought entered my mind. "I'm a writer," I said meekly. A desperate look set on Snyderman's face. I really felt for the guy.

Not a single teacher showed up. On normal days, a thousand kids attend Moore. On this day 200 youngsters checked in. Kindergarten and first grade were dismissed. Ten parent volunteers and four substitutes arrived for "combat" duty. I was the eleventh, inducted unceremoniously into classroom 217.

My fourth graders consisted of 17 children, five whites and 12 black youngsters. The boy who became my biggest discipline problem turned out to be the most gifted artist in the classroom. He was also the poorest reader.

What my super-charged eight and nine-year-olds accomplished in the next six hours would hardly make worth-while reading in an educational journal. At times I felt the classroom was being turned into a missile base for flying spitballs. Most of the 12 boys in the class behaved like cannonballs, up and out of their seats every two minutes. They went to the bathroom so often I got the distinct impression the lavatory had become the venue for a floating crap game.

My first mistake was trying to teach fourth graders from the side of the room sitting at a desk. Snyderman came in and suggested politely that I stand at the front of the class.

"More control that way," he smiled encouragingly. Then he walked out. *Control.* That's what was lacking here, I decided. And that's how I stumbled onto what turned out to be a somewhat successful method of quieting restless feet. Suddenly I saw my role transformed from cop to teacher.

The key: Fun and games. I divided the class into four teams for spelling and reading exercises. They were permitted to choose their own captains and the team with the lowest point score won. The idea caught fire.

Kids who previously were unable or unwilling to read words like "stars" and "drum" were now anxious to win a pocketful of candy for their team. The spitballs quieted and ceased.

At noon I brought home Kevin and Donald because they forgot their bags on the school bus. It was my hope that the strike would end over the weekend. If not, I was faced with a potential domestic crisis: How would my wife react when I brought home 17 hungry boys for lunch?

29

Before Bandstand

In 1952 a mop-haired 16-year-old West Catholic High School junior with a big pompadour made what he considers some kind of history in Philadelphia. And, after all, why not? The Quaker City is a storehouse of American history.

What distinguished Don Flanagan is that he was the first *record runner* for the TV show that became the forerunner to *American Bandstand*.

By his own admission Flanagan told me, he was not much of a dancer. But as for girls, he says, "I loved them." And so he signed up to show up Monday through Fridays at the old home of WFIL-TV at 46th and Market Streets. Flanagan, tall, a string bean of a kid, was given the assignment to run records from the station's afternoon teen record hop with Lee Stewart and Bob Horn across the hall to the radio station. He deposited them into the hands of a young 26-year old from upstate New York. His name was Dick Clark.

"No, they didn't pay me," Flanagan laughed. "But every once in awhile, Dick Clark would interview me over the air. And I would tell him what it was like meeting Patti Page, Danny and The Juniors, and the Four Aces. I fell in love with Teresa Brewer."

Then Flanagan would race back to the TV studio where he and his *Committee of Nine* were tasked with keeping the hordes of descending teens at bay from Most Blessed Sacrament and West Catholic High. Flanagan said he and his girls managed to keep things orderly by distributing color coded entry tickets, each assigned for a different day of the week. For the record, I can tell you I was among those hordes. Teenagers mobbed the studios, flocking in from schools all over the city.

I remember one well-endowed young lady who stood at the entrance to the studios. When the checker beckoned for her pass, she offered a snarky response I'll never forget: "This is my pass," she giggled, unbuttoning her blouse. The teen got in.

Outside, a fight erupted between two young guys waiting in the long line snaking around Market Street. The confrontation became bloody and police were summoned. My Wednesday pass worked like magic. Inside the studios it was chaotic despite the flickering *On The Air* sign. I never returned.

It was Bob Horn who is credited with establishing much of the basic format of the later incarnation of *American Bandstand*. A week before the fall school year in 1952, Horn met with WFIL Station Manager George Koehler. Horn was invited to move his WPEN program onto TV. The deal required that Horn co-host the show with Lee Stewart.

Stewart — short, squat with dark, horn-rimmed glasses — was the glue that kept Bandstand afloat. He was the pitchman for Mad Mad Muntz TV, the lynchpin that became Bandstand's first sponsor. The playbook for the original show went like this: A few records would be aired. Horn would introduce some guests. Film clips of music videos would follow. The format was a flop.

From the start, Horn was unhappy with the film-based program. He sought to have it changed to teens dancing along live on camera. His vision was based on WPEN's highly successful *950 Club*, hosted by Joe Grady and Ed Hurst. The *Bandstand* makeover debuted on October 7, 1952. Hundreds of teens turned out to dance on live TV often drawing over 60 percent of the daytime audience.

Flanagan, now 83, lives in Sevierville, TN, a stone's throw from Dolly Parton's Dollywood. Don told me he remembers Stewart as friendly and congenial. Horn, he recalls, was "standoffish, with a kind of self-important air." After 18 months, Flanagan says he could no longer take the harassment from his schoolmates at West Catholic. "They called me *Mr. Bandstand*. So I quit."

Horn was fired in 1956 after a drunk driving arrest. He was also charged and later acquitted of statutory rape with a teenage girl. Clark replaced him after a period of on-air tryouts from other DJs.

In the end, Clark transformed himself and WFIL-TV into two of the most culturally significant forces of the early rock-and-roll era. New elements that became part of its trademark, included the high school gym-like bleachers and the famous segment in which teenage studio guests rated the newest records on a scale from 25 to 98. The teens offered such criticisms as "It's got a good beat, and you can dance to it."

The heart of *American Bandstand* always remained the sound of the day's most popular music combined with the sight of the show's unpolished teen "regulars" dancing and showing off the latest fashions in clothing and hairstyles. Clark's iconic show, *American Bandstand*, began broadcasting nationally in 1957, beaming images to 67 ABC affiliates. What viewers saw was clean-cut, average teenagers dancing to the not-so-clean-cut Jerry Lee Lewis' *Whole Lotta Shakin Goin' On*. In 1963 the show moved to Los Angeles and began a 24-year run as a taped weekly program with Dick Clark as host.

So what happened to Don Flanagan? Don graduated from West Catholic, went to work for a construction company and for the next 20 years served in the Navy. "I wanted to go to Vietnam," he told me. "But, instead, they sent me to Hawaii and Spain."

30

Lessons Learned

Those I met and interviewed over the years — both the famous and even the infamous — offered me some important lessons.

Here is my list:

- **Mother Teresa** taught me that without a purpose, my life, my career would never be fulfilled. She helped me realize that a return to journalism — to chasing bad guys and bad institutions — would recharge my batteries. It did.
- Presidential wannabe **Ted Kennedy** taught me that it's possible to do great things even in the face of great tragedy.
- **Jackie Gleason**, in his haste for my departure, taught me again the virtues of patience even though the Great One manifested none.

- **George Martorano,** the son of a Philadelphia Mafia kingpin, spent 32 years behind bars for his refusal to testify against his father. Once named *Prisoner of the Year,* he was ultimately released from a federal penitentiary. Over the years Mortorano helped in the rehabilitation of hundreds of his jail mates. And from a jail cell, wrote several books. We all deserve second chances.
- **Martin Luther King**'s sacrifice taught me the lesson of fearlessness. His message to me was to stand up to villains of every stripe. Those who judge based on race, religion, sex, age, disability, and gender orientation.
- **Bipin Shah,** the architect behind the MAC machine, recovered his missing daughters after a $3.4 million world-wide manhunt. Shah taught me that even the toughest odds can be overcome. Requirements: time, patience and an abundance of financial resources.
- **Joe Frazier** taught me the gift of generosity. After a whirlwind campaign to promote a local bank he penned these words on a boxing glove gifted to me: "To Ed Eisen … Boogie Boogie. Joe Frazier." The Tuff-Wear trophy still sits on my bookcase since his defeat by George Foreman in 1973.
- **John McCandlish Phillips** is the remarkable *New York Times* reporter who kept a King James Bible on the edge of his desk. My friend reminded me that whenever you're in need of courage, answers to the unanswerable — God's word is the place to go.

- **John Forbes Nash, Jr.** the brilliant mathematician on whose life the movie *A Beautiful Mind* was based, taught me that the stigma of mental illness requires deletion from the American psyche.

- **Bill Schwabe**, the German-born immigrant who came to America to escape Hitler, began his career as a dishwasher. He later went on to become Human Resources Director at one of the nation's top medical hospitals. He gives me hope that in America ... still anything is possible.

About The Author

Ed Eisen's career in communications spans 52 years. He is a Freedoms Foundation recipient and an award-winning journalist at three major metropolitan newspapers including The *Philadelphia Inquirer,* a broadcast news reporter and public relations consultant where his clients included two popes and a world-boxing champion. He taught broadcast news journalism at Temple University and crafted hundreds of profiles on the famous, the infamous and the faceless in society. Ed has worked as a volunteer ESL teacher for over two decades and serves as a board member of two non-profit community service organizations: Broadcast Pioneers of Philadelphia and the Rotary Club of Willow Grove, PA. He speaks frequently at schools, historical associations, libraries, churches, synagogues, and retirement communities.

Index

41st International Eucharistic Congress, 55
Archdiocese of Philadelphia, 55
Babush, Dick, 11, 33
Baldini, Bill, 80
Bandstand, 123-125
Bar Mitzvah, 37
Broderick, Gov. Raymond, 81
Brooklyn, 17
Burros, Daniel, 22
Camden Courier Post, 12
Camden High School, 31
Carter, President Jimmy, 92
City Cleaning Co., 16
Clark, Dick, 123
Cohen, George, 16
Connelly, Jennifer, 76
Crowe, Russell, 76
Cuba, 29
Deep Throat, 79
Delaware Valley Florists Association, 20
Edmund Pettus Bridge, 84
Eisen, Bill, 15, 52, 56
Eisen, Ed, 47, 49
Eisen, Marion, 38, 41
Eisen, Seth, 43
Eisen, Stephen, 44, 51

Ellis Island, 15, 26
Facenda, John, 80, 115
Feldstein, Stacy, 48
Ferrell, David, 56
Flanagan, Don, 123
Ford, President Gerald, 55
Foreman, George, 72
Frazier, Joe, 45, 71, 128
Freedoms Foundation, 131
Ft. Lauderdale News, 18
Germantown Savings Bank, 71
Gleason, Jackie, 87-89, 127
Gold, Gwen, 42
Gray & Rogers, 71
Harper-Collins, 44
Held, Leo, 111-112
Hoover, J. Edgar, 85
Horn, Bob, 124-125
Jesus, 33, 38
Johns Hopkins Hospital, 25
Jorgensen, Christine, 101, 103
Kelly, Princess Grace, 55
Kennedy, Edward M., 91, 93, 127
King, Rev. Martin Luther, 83-85, 128
Koch, Mayor Edward, 109
Kopechne, Mary Jo, 91-93
Ku Klux Klan, 21

Life Magazine, 93
Lindberg, Charles, 67
Lopez, Steve, 69
Mafia, 63
Menotti, Carlo, 29
Messiah, 44
Messianic Jews, 33
Mishpocha, 41
Missionaries of Charity, 59
Mortorano, Ralph, 63, 128
Mortorano, Paul, 63, 128
Mother Teresa, 46, 59, 127
Nasar, Sylvia, 76
Nash, John Forbes Jr., 75-77, 129
National Center for Missing and Exploited Children, 68
New Testament Fellowship, 22
New York Times, 21
Orthodox Jew, 37
Pennhurst State School and Hospital, 29
Pennsylvania State Publishers Association, 19
Philadelphia Bulletin, 17-18, 61
Philadelphia Inquirer, 14, 18, 83, 107
Phillips, John McCandlish, 48, 128
Pope John Paul II, 57
Pope Paul VI, 55
Public Relations Consultant, 20
Reynolds, Charles, 19
Roberts, John, 115-118
Roman Catholic Church, 55
Saint of the Gutters, 59-61
Schwabe, Bill, 25, 129

Shah, Bipin, 19, 67-69, 128
Stanton, Dr. Gerald, 38
Steigler, Herbert, 95-97
Taub, Allen, 79
Temple University, 16, 116
The Atlantic City Press, 19
The Fort Lauderdale News, 87
TIME Magazine, 69
Tischer, Edna, 29
Tischer, Joan, 29, 33
Tischer, Sam, 29, 33
University of Pennsylvania, 26
USA Today, 68
Vietnam War, 84
WCAM Radio, 14
WCAU-TV, 28
WFIL-TV, 123
WRTI Radio, 115

CPSIA information can be obtained
at www.ICGtesting.com
Printed in the USA
BVHW032245071019
560494BV00001B/7/P